For Jo Lee

Soar like an eagle
To the highest mountain top
Prepare to take flight

Chez Ann

Acknowledgements

Bobby - my love, my heart, thank-you

Michelle - I am blessed

To my editor Alex Mitchell, thank you for your kind help.

Thank you to my muses - Sara Teasdale and Emily Dickinson

EMOTIVE

Poetry to awaken the senses
&
soothe the soul

Chez Ann

EMOTIVE
Author –Cheryl Ann Flynn

© Cheryl Flynn 2016

This book is sold with the understanding that the author is not offering specific personal advice to the reader. For professional advice, seek the services of a suitable, qualified practitioner. The author disclaims any responsibility for liability, loss or risk, personal or otherwise, that happens as a consequence of the use and application of any of the contents of this book.

All rights reserved. This book may not be reproduced in whole or part, stored, posted on the internet, or transmitted in any form or by any means, electronic, mechanical, photocopying, recording, or other, without permission from the author of this book.

Editing by: Alex Fullerton www.authorsupportservices.com
Design by: Sylvie Blair www.bookpod.com.au
Printed and Bound in Australia by: Ingram

National Library of Australia Cataloguing-in-Publication entry
Creator: Chez Ann, author.
Title: Emotive : poetry to awaken the senses and soothe the soul / Chez Ann ; edited by Alex Fullerton.
ISBN: 9780994162984 (paperback)
Subjects: Australian poetry.
Other Creators/Contributors:
Fullerton, Alex J. L., editor.
Dewey Number: A821.4

Contents

Introduction 9
Beauty 11
Winter Dawn 13
Heart 15
My Dog 17
Life Is 19
Full Moon 21
Forever More 23
Drunken Love 25
Old Man 27
Old Woman 29
Shelter 31
Flood 33
Take Flight 35
Waning 37
Remember When 39
Loss 41
Haiku 43
Our Children 45
Flame Robin 47
Feelings 49
Guitar Strum 51
Emotive 53

Dear Reader,

Welcome.

It is a privilege to share my poetry. It would be an honour if you added *Emotive* to your collection of special books, or you may wish to gift it to somebody you love.

We all experience a kaleidoscope of feeling in life. It is what makes us human. *Emotive* covers some of these themes, including love, loss, happiness, loneliness, isolation and ageing.

I have always found peace and inspiration through immersing myself in reading and writing verse, which I have used as a form of self-therapy since the age of sixteen.

Emotive was written from the heart to emote a feeling of comfort. We humans are all different and unique but the one thing we have in common is that we all experience feelings. Poetry, music and books enable us to connect on that level.

Social networking also enables us to connect on an emotional level and since the 90s we have been lucky to incorporate the use of fun emoticons (emotive icons) in our communications on Facebook and text messages to convey more feeling and the intended tone. I think most of us appreciate receiving a text accompanied with a big smiley face blowing a kiss...

I hope *Emotive* awakens your senses and soothes your soul.

> "After great pain, a formal feeling comes.
> The nerves sit ceremonious, like tombs"
> Emily Dickinson

EMOTIVE

The street is lined with a canopy of trees
An umbrella of elm and jacaranda
Leaves whirl and pirouette in the breeze
Scent of salty sea and coastal banksia
When young, she froze this day in her memory
To melt like ice when needing serenity
Eighteen then and turning heads with her beauty
Days so enchanting remain a rarity
She tries to remember time and time again
Like a shooting star it happens now and then
Where certain scents spark a feeling, heaven sent
And she time-travels back to younger days spent
Her past and present become one and align
Where salty sea breezes are familiar
Summer memories as sweet as clementine
She was as pretty as bougainvillea
Hot sand burns her feet running to the seashore
Past the man singing reggae, wearing dreadlocks
She had the whole world in her hands to explore
Striking as London plane trees, Queensland brush box
A silk kaftan snakes round her slender body
Scent of citrus and hot northerly winds blow
Eighteen then and turning heads with her beauty
A vision amongst the Archipelago

Beauty

EMOTIVE

Rain bucketing down proud
Lazy Sunday sleep in

Choir of frogs singing loud
Lorikeets echoing

Sun cracks bright yellow yolk
Woven through the grey sky

Chatter of the town folk
Aroma...coffee...pie

Hours continue to swarm
Like bees to elegant wattle

As we while away the dawn
Elegantly horizontal

Carpe Diem! Seize the day
A brushstroke of yellow on grey

Winter Dawn

EMOTIVE

Words are obsolete
Beat...beat...beat...beat...beat
Oh my heart aching
Tingling head to feet

Numbness conquers speech
You are out of reach
Love-filled blood coursing
Heart a hungry leech

Heart will surrender
Oh make my heart sing
Heart is a drummer
Rhythmically pounding

Heart

♒

EMOTIVE

Perched at the riverbank, my dog for company
Two solitary lighthouses stare out to sea
So undisturbed and still you can see a tide drop
Traders yet to put out signs, open up their shop

Two mushrooms hiding in shadow of an oak tree
As sunrise stirs awake the day's calamity
A seagull's squawk talks over the tranquillity
As he devours chips discarded from last night's tea

The river ripples a darker blue than the sky
Fishermen take advantage of tide that is high
Rainbow lorikeets engage animatedly
Foraging for nectar from an umbrella tree

Bold kites cling to keen kite surfers taking a chance
Bop to and fro to the rhythm of the wind's dance.
Bakery opens and his tail wags knowingly
Our mouths drool as we eye our favourite pastry.

My Dog

EMOTIVE

Life is a sea, with varied tides and currents
Life is a wave, swept away with occurrence

Life is a cruise ship, voyaging, yours to steer
Life is a pirate, ahoy there, have no fear

Life is a tide when low you can feel alone
Remember that kin are a sea journey home

Life tides ebb, when they are high you feel content
Seashells echo ocean tales: sweet travels dreamt

Life Is

EMOTIVE

The moon is a naked lychee, full and plump
A lantern that shimmers a path out to sea

My soul hurtles outward into a high jump
Soars across the ocean to eternity

Full Moon

?

EMOTIVE

When I am down and am out
Wondering what if? And why?
Remember we both did try
Kiss good-bye sad lullaby

Need a compatible love
One to share the ups and downs
Away from the city lights
To faraway charming towns

When I am down and am out
I will find my true soul mate
Together forever more
Side by side at Heaven's gate

Forever More

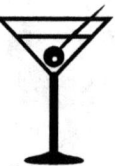

EMOTIVE

Takes a sip, a toke and drag
Friday night 'tis the life led
Bull out the gate vexed red rag
Drinking until off your head

Yet we know nobody leads
And nobody to follow
He says one more, no she pleads
Feeling empty and hollow

Harsh inaudible waffle
Noisy unclear jabbering
One drop left in the bottle
Vitriolic blabbering

Drunken love we shan't sustain
God spare us this affliction
Pray, go to AA, refrain
Bottle full of addiction

Drunken Love

EMOTIVE

Take a look at the withered old man
He has withstood a long life journey
Enduring much, this we understand

Every wrinkle written on his face
Is like a road map of his travels
Navigating through the human race

Look deep into his wise older eyes
Eyes like rough diamonds cut and polished
Glint and sparkle till the day he dies

Where will he go journey's end, closed eyes?
Drift to a place, journey to heaven
Dance with choir of angels at sunrise

Old Man

EMOTIVE

I still hold this youthful girl inside
I caress her arms as I close my eyes
Beneath the wrinkles she still does hide
Remembering her sensual thighs

Remembering her slender girth
Sagging of bosom as I towel dry
Remembering that they once were pert
When bikinis did not make her shy

Old woman do not be so anxious
Old woman, underneath you're the same
Hidden beneath the wrinkled canvas
A stunning portrait you shall remain

Old Woman

EMOTIVE

Homeless woman sits; her cup of coffee is empty
Charade, make-believing it overflows aplenty

Her eyes hold mine, captive awhile, then darting to and fro
Pretend not to notice she has nowhere else to go

I shan't acknowledge her bottomless cup of coffee
Nor the mismatch of shoes she wears, one black, one toffee

Nor the dirt dug deep into her cat-like fingernails
Clawing at her lifeline as outside it rains and hails

I feign indifference re-join my conversation
With an air of ignorance - that will never be me

Deep down having a disturbing realisation
Homelessness a pay cheque away from my reality

Billions are living homeless in abject poverty
Recession, job loss, squalor, living in tent city

Homelessness is increasing, slum areas depressed
Homeless lass, you and I, shelter from the rain
God bless

Shelter

EMOTIVE

The sea is a carpet
Rolling over the sand

Spills down the escarpment
Treading over the land

Rain is hammering down
Streets are shag pile rivers

Water lies upon town
Earth is cold, it shivers

News broadcast, flood warning
Life is lost, washed away

Alas, global warming
Willows weep; we all pray

Flood

EMOTIVE

Another Sunday night
I wish I could escape
Like a bird and take flight
Fly over the landscape

Escape feeling empty
Escape feeling hollow
Hands trembling sweaty
Escape bleak tomorrow

Subliminal doctrine
Plays over in my head
Tomorrow's sold, auctioned
While I take leave in bed

I dread to face the dawn
Flying birds face no scorn

Take Flight

EMOTIVE

I am
a face
Look for
a place
Peer through
windows
A face
No blame
Hide head
in shame
When you
see face
Waning
Moon face
Yearn for
embrace
No more
misplace
Kindred
cosy
Fireplace

Waning

EMOTIVE

Remember when it was simple, so clear
A precious time, free from pain and fear

We played, talked and dreamt of what we'd become
Danced to Roxette, Kylie and Prince albums

So young and brave, we felt invincible
A time of learning and living simple

Together we vowed to remain this way
Life drifts; memories buoy our yesterday

Remember chasing after our future
Dreamt to be grown ups and having our say

The years roll on; the present comes so fast
Recollect our fruitful and sacred past

Remember When

EMOTIVE

As the rain pelts down
Gate opens, floods sky
I watch with a frown
Bid sunshine good-bye

You no longer lead
Sit out the tango
No flax to my seed
A flameless candle

We were synchronised
We have lost the sync
Two vines once entwined
Missing chain in link

Once close now estranged
A new perspective
Parallel now changed
Twin, disconnected

Spa with no bubble
Body without soul
Trouble, no double
Burden taking toll

Tears stream down my face
Tears of crying eye
Loss hard to replace
You bid me good-bye

Loss

EMOT**IVE**

Joining together
Branching out with open limbs
Intertwined tree roots

Bird egg falls from nest
Nature has her own timing
Chirpy hatchling fly

As the rain pelts down
Below the heavenly sky
Bid sunshine good-bye

Leaves falling from tree
A peaceful breeze flowing through
Unattached and free

Haiku

EMOTIVE

All I think of is our children
Our country that they will grow in

We hold responsibility
From our cities to vast country

The world is out there to explore
Take a flight from Oz to Singapore

Then the world is outside your door
A big kid in a candy store

Mountains, rivers to the seashore
Canada, Spain to East Timor

So many countries to explore
Take a flight from Oz to Singapore

Encourage all children to see
Australia as family

The world a neighbour and a friend
Whose good tidings we shall extend

Colour of rainbow we unite
New generation peace in sight

Our Children

EMOTIVE

Hibernating away like a grizzly bear
She'd been reluctant to leave her comfy chair
She had been reclusive all the winter long
Till spring brought the serenade of his sweet song

A robin visited her every spring day
He'd tap the windowsill till she looked his way
Though she had work to do and deadlines to meet
She could no longer ignore him singing so sweet

Her monochrome life he'd turned into colour
He taught her there was life yet to discover
His sweet song beckoned her to venture outside
She felt peaceful and life became simplified

She watched as he glided up into the sky
Then as he swooped back down, to her, to say hi
He would flap his wings and display his red chest
Insects he would catch and take back to his nest

Flame robin kept singing his favourite tune
She observed him until the late afternoon
He took pride in her watching him sing and play
Left her at dusk to attend a bird soiree

Flame Robin

EMOTIVE

Your personality is bottled within
Be an individual and love your skin
Open up your heart and let your love flow
Learn new things and don't be afraid to grow

If you ask what will life bring you tomorrow?
The answer may be happiness or sorrow
Life can bring feelings that are hard to share
Feelings of loneliness and of despair

At times you may feel you don't know who you are
When love is too hard and distant as a star
Know you hold the key to unlock your soul
Where love inside your heart will make you whole

Feelings

EMOTIVE

Firelight flickers through the curtain
He strums his favourite ovation guitar

Which song I cannot be certain
He has an audience of twinkling stars

The tunes he plays are lyrical
Rhythmic beats, eclectic sounds of Creole

Strums an upbeat original
As he stokes the dancing fire and my soul

Guitar Strum

EMOTIVE

Nothing untoward had come from what she wrote
Except that one time writing a fake sick note
She ended up with a detention at school
And learnt that words could be a powerful tool

Next foray she wrote for a competition
A written verse about bank fraud prevention
Chose a verb, a noun and subordinate word
Won first prize and her voice was finally heard

A poet's emotive words bring much feeling
Some words written and spoken cut like a knife
Others make your heart soar out to the ceiling
Words chosen carefully have brought her no strife

At times her words are spoken as tongue in cheek
It's cathartic to write words she cannot speak
Words like I love you never lose their power
Speed to your heart at one hundred km/hour

She texts her friends adding cool emoticons
Nice to share words with emotion and icon
Used since the 90s for social networking
Smileys convey her intended tone, feeling

Prose read till the curtain of new day is drawn
Till the words of yesterday are dead and gone
Dot her i, cross her t till her novel ends
Words used wisely bring you no trouble my friends

Emotive

About the Author

Chez Ann grew up in Melbourne and began writing verse as a sixteen year old, finding solace in expressing her feelings through poetry. She enjoys listening to song lyrics and reading poetry by Emily Dickinson and Sara Teasdale, exploring the true meaning and intended tone of the words. She now resides in Queensland with her husband and beloved dog. *Emotive*, her first published book of poems was written to emote a sense of connectedness, a comfort in dealing with the kaleidoscope of feelings common to many of us. Chez Ann wrote *Emotive* to open your senses and soothe your soul as much as hers.

www.ingramcontent.com/pod-product-compliance
Lightning Source LLC
Chambersburg PA
CBHW070552300426
44113CB00011B/1882